T0068953

This Long Winter

Books by Joyce Sutphen

Straight Out of View
Coming Back to the Body
Naming the Stars
Fourteen Sonnets
First Words
House of Possibility
After Words
Modern Love & Other Myths
The Green House
Carrying Water to the Field: New and Selected Poems
This Long Winter

This Long Winter

Joyce Sutphen

The Cox Family Poetry Chapbook Series

Carnegie Mellon University Press
Pittsburgh 2022

Acknowledgments

This Long Winter by Joyce Sutphen is the third volume in The Cox Family Poetry Chapbook Series of Carnegie Mellon University Press. The Press administrators and staff express their profound appreciation to Courtney, Lisa, and Jordan Cox for their generous support.

Book design by Trevor Lazar

ISBN 978-0-88748-678-4
Printed in the United States of America

10   9   8   7   6   5   4   3   2   1

Library of Congress Cataloging-in-Publication Data
Names: Sutphen, Joyce, author.
Title: *This Long Winter* / Joyce Sutphen.
Description: Pittsburgh : Carnegie Mellon University Press, 2022. | Series:
    The Cox family poetry chapbook series ; 3 | Summary: "*This Long Winter*
    contains poems that are meditations on life in the rural world: reflections
    on hard work, aging, and the ravages of time-erasures that Sutphen
    attempts to ameliorate with her careful attention to language. These poems
    move us from delight in precise description to wisdom and solace in the
    things of this world. Noticing its details, the snowflakes, clementines, the
    lilies, the cardinal's call, is the key for this momentary stay against time that
    comes at us in a rush. The many mirror images in these poems point to the
    complexity and hard, loving work of really living in the world. And now, in
    the deep mid-winter, deep in the enforced slowdown of this pandemic, we
    need these poems to help us know what to do with the past and how to live
    and how to love" —Provided by publisher.
Identifiers: LCCN 2021044804 | ISBN 9780887486784 (trade paperback)
Subjects: LCGFT: Poetry.
Classification: LCC PS3569.U857 L66 2022 | DDC 811/.54--dc23
LC record available at https://lccn.loc.gov/2021044804

Contents

First Snow

I was at my desk, thinking,
which caused me to miss
the first snow that fell
on the still green bush
outside my window.

And then I looked up
to see a steady fall
of faintest white already
covering the roof
across the street.

It was so slight a snow
it seemed that there
was nothing in the air
until it made of everything
a page as blank as this.

The Bright Obvious

As predicted, it stood there in the morning
bright and clear, although the question we asked

was gone now, and the air was much colder—
rain turned to ice. I made a list . . . coffee too.

I thought about the birds at the feeder last week:
pairs of cardinals, blue jays, woodpeckers,

dozens of chickadees, and sparrows. Where do
the birds go when the wind shakes the branches

like a housemaid with a rug? Perhaps
I should say the obvious thing now—

something like it seems we've lost our way,
and now, I notice the first new snowflakes

and how bright they are as they fill the air,
how soon they will cover everything.

On the Longest Day

I fall out of orbit. I falter and fail.
My heart is not a constant clock;
it is not as steadfast as iron.
If you burn me, I will melt.

Up to my old tricks again, I bargain
with the light: "Oh, let him think of me
before the sun goes down"—and then:
"Or before the sky is dark."

I would have known, without being told
that today is the longest day of the year.
More time for the birds to whittle
away the sky, more time for the wind

in the willow branches. I would have
known this circling of the year, even
if no one ever mentioned it—that
even the planet must tilt and turn.

Things That Have to Happen

I'm eating a pear and watching the snow
mix with the green grass and the yellow leaves
on the birch tree across the street. Tonight
I am going to hear a poet read.

There are things right with the world, despite all
the wrongness. A father knocks at the door
of a crack house looking for his oldest
son, and years later that boy is talking

on the radio as I drive home from
the reading, which was as beautiful
as the cover of her book. Remember,
she says, when no one ever locked the door

and the only thing worth stealing might be
a bicycle or a pair of shoes. Imagine how much
we don't need to have. Imagine how hard
it is to be our children, all that weight

bending them down before they learn to fly.
Finally, the boy had to give it up
or it was going to kill him. Sometimes,
like winter, there are things that have to happen.

Such Courage

Li Po the little boat is gone
        —W. S. Merwin

Once, in London, on the Hungerford Bridge,
I wondered if all of time existed

at once, and when I looked up, I saw it did,
and once, in Boulder, Colorado, when I

was drowning in sorrow, I asked for love
and it came into me like a river.

In Chatham, New Jersey, I asked for a sign:
if one thing happened, I'd do this, and if

another thing happened, I'd do that. No. Yes.
I used to ask the moon to lead me home.

I'd ask the stars to show me what to wish;
wherever the wind was blowing, I'd ask

for a ride—I used to have such courage.

Solstice

for Louis Jenkins

The earth is tilted
as far away from

the sun as it can go.
The longest nights

pass like tall ships
on an endless ocean.

We hear nothing, and
then we hear that you

have stopped eating,
that you are fading.

Oh fierce and beautiful
friend! The sun hangs

low on the horizon,
the shadows are long.

I think of how the light
always returns, how

this time you will be
on the other side of it

with the sun and
the moon and stars.

Only Yesterday

Without me, the house sits empty
on the edge of the marsh;
deer walk through the yard
leaving a trail in the snow.

At the grocery store, I buy bread
and coffee, apples and clementines.
White wine. When I come home,
I open a box of music and fill

the place with piano and cello.
Later, when I cry out in my sleep
there is no one to wake. All night
I wander from room to room questioning:

Why haven't I read Lucretius and
Basho? Shouldn't I know at least one
more language? What was I doing
as time filled my skin with wrinkles?

Wasn't it only yesterday for everything?

Between the Stars

For a long time, we went on living.
We were casual about it—not wanting

to draw attention to our good fortune.
We asked so little of the universe—

only that it leave us alone, that it
pass us over this year and then the next.

After a while, we seemed invincible.
When our bodies began to betray us,

we were as surprised as they were, looking
into mirrors at faces we didn't

recognize. Now the distance between the stars
mattered to us, and now it didn't. Time,

as always, was the villain, with his scythe
and crooked knife. Oh, how we hated him!

In Winter

How old I am tonight,
winding the moonlight through my hair,
sifting the sand with my bones.

Reading your words through bleary eyes,
it all seems so far away, proverbs
for someone I'll never be.

"Bodily decrepitude is wisdom," one said.
"Don't be afraid," said another.
Tomorrow I will write letters—

one to a man who folds the morning
into a poem, and one to a woman
who is losing her way.

What can I say? I know how useless it is to
thread the stars with worry. "Consider the lilies,"
she said. "I do," I said. . . . Then what?

Blue

I was waiting for the future,
expecting it to arrive as it

always had, slipping into place
at the very last moment, just

in time to answer the roll call.
"Here," it would say, "as always,"

until one day it would arrive
so late that it would become

the past, and there it would be
forever after that, and nothing

more could happen in the here
and now, where we find ourselves

this morning, that place between
the past and future, where (if

only we could see it) everything
is happening at once, or (if

you prefer) there's only the
morning sky with its golden

clouds dissolving into blue.

Tell Me

Tell me, again, how it was—
how we used to go away for weeks

at a time, staying in someone's house
(someone who was far away, staying

in some other person's house),
and how we ate breakfast wandering

through the markets, and when the
museums opened, we'd be in the Prado

going from Velázquez to Goya until
we found *The Garden of Earthly Delights.*

Tell me how we used to go out
in the evening to the theater, where

real people acted upon a stage
in front of rows and rows of people,

how this happened every night, how
we packed into the trains, going from

stop to stop with people who left no trace,
how our bodies still were fortresses

against the diseases of those days.
Tell me again how it was.

Blessing the World

I mean the one that surrounds us,
the one that causes such suffering
and refuses to let us go. I mean
that one,

and the one full of stupidity—the one
that some of us scroll endlessly
doom-raged and cursing—that one
especially.

I mean what world we have left
once we have covered the meadows
with housing developments
and strip malls;

I mean the poor ruined earth
beneath our deals and our markets
where everything has a price
even here,

even now—which is why
we must bless it with the part of us
that made the music and the paintings,
the bridges, airplanes, and the dictionaries

where the word for what we will do
has not yet been invented.

The Moon in the Mirror

I like how I can see the moon
and the tree inside the window
reflected in the mirror.

The whole world is in there—
even my face looking up
from the bed where I was sleeping

until the bright moon slipped
from the highest branch and
woke me without a sound.

I try to watch the moon and the
tree in the mirror that reflects
the window looking out across

the snowy yard. Even when I
know where I am, I am surprised
to see how the moon comes

so close to earth, and makes
her face as smooth as glass,
as shiny as a silver mirror.

Snow Falling

Months before and months after he died
I could barely write a word, mouth
full of echoes and stone.

Everything I started stalled on the page—
experiments in flight that failed,
ships that sank in the harbor.

Now I wander from one room to another,
looking out at the marsh, at the blue
shadows falling across the yard.

I always knew he would die someday,
but I didn't believe it. When I look up
again, the snow is falling—

it drifts and turns in the air, as if
it would cover the whole world—
graves and all.

Get Back

It's going to take more than an address
and a phone number. It will mean

many wrong turns and endless detours.
All of the words you learned? Forgotten—

along with the grammar and history
of that tongue. As for plot?

That always evaded you, didn't it?
Once you'd taken that first wrong turn,

it became impossible to get back to
the road you were meant to be traveling.

Towns changed and there were different
people in them; the weather didn't wait

for you to happen under the sky.
You will have to learn how to tell time

again, but after a while everything
will be of the moment, present, and

accounted for. You will undo the damage
that was done; you will know the voice

when it calls; you will even know
how to tell the dancer from the dance.

The Detail

This morning, it was the digital smile
on the radio, the space-needle
rings on the water bottle,

and every winter branch in the dawning
sky, the cardinal's call
as certain as it is red,

words on a page, the loveliness of
letters lining up together, changing
places, as in a dance.

Meaning is in the detail. If you pay
attention, I tell her, that
will be enough.

The Owl

I hear it for a while before I hear it;
that is, before I realize I'm hearing

a bird call from deep in the woods behind
the house across the street. It's an owl—

a barred owl—I guess, making the familiar
"Who cooks for you, who cooks for you" call.

If I could see her, I'd see her head swivel
a half circle just before she leans in

and pushes out that cry, one more time. I've
just finished reading Brecht's question about

the dark times and the answer: "Yes, there will
be singing. About the dark times." Why do

these somewhat bitter words make me smile?
Why do I lift my head, shake my hair free,

and leap to my feet, clapping my hands together?

Amaryllis

This is the message I want to bring:
everything breaking into beauty.

Green shoot climbing the empty air,
opening in a profusion—

how well you negotiate with time,
there at the castle gates.

Force or flower, neither and both,
each cluster of trumpets blaring,

already I know the answer;
it came in the expected way.

One thing dies so another can live.
You are old, you should know that.

Still Listening

Tonight, I could go to bed with
the sunset reflecting on the windows
of the house across the street,
the deer still grazing in the marsh,

or tonight, I could stay up late,
listening to the BBC long after
the windows turn black
and the deer, shoulder to shoulder,

sleep in their nest—those four young ones
I watched from the kitchen, their luminous
ears twitching, their bodies dark
against the tall sun-bleached grass.

Tonight, listening to in-between radio—
Sonny Rollins talking about finding
that last chord, and Billie Holiday singing "East
of the Sun (West of the Moon),"

I decide that I might stay up all night,
or as long as Louis Armstrong is singing
"New Orleans Stomp" (ham and greens), his
trumpet blowing over the stride piano

and drums, a clarinet twirling a ribbon
up and down the scat singer's
happy song—which is when I remember
you for the first time this long winter,

and wish I could call to let you know
that I'm still listening to every note.

Burning

I wrote a poem
that began in ecstasy—

no gradual buildup
into horn blaring Bolero,

no slow twist turning into
whirling dervish—

unless you count the hours
of practice, the silent rooms

of poets imagining
a way to become the dance,

a glance brightening in
a lover's eyes, someone

who has waited an eternity
to ascend without a ticket

or a gown, her empty lamp
burning, burning, burning.

Books in the Cox Family Poetry Chapbook Series

2021
Elegiac, Charles Seluzicki

2022
What Passes Here for Mountains, Matt Morton
This Long Winter, Joyce Sutphen